PLANTAIN COOKBOOK

Tomi Makanjuola

www.vegannigerian.com

PLANTAIN COOKBOOK

Tomi Makanjuola

www.vegannigerian.com

For my family

Plantain Cookbook by Tomi Makanjuola

First published in Great Britain in 2018

Text © Tomi Makanjuola
Cover photograph © Sofia Popov
Portrait photographs © Sofia Popov
Food photographs © Tomi Makanjuola

Ebook, soft and hard cover copies available via:
www.vegannigerian.com
Amazon.co.uk
Blurb.co.uk

Contents

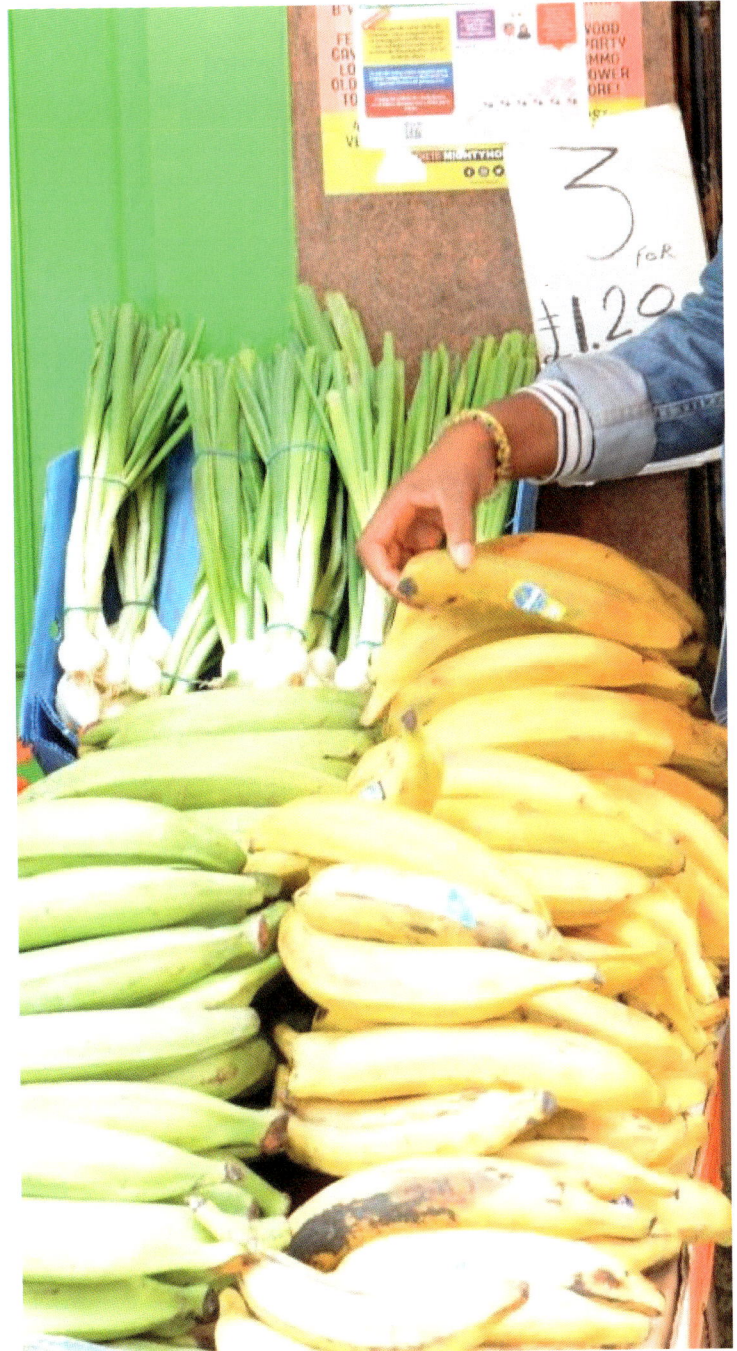

Introduction

What is your earliest memory of plantain? Perhaps, like me, plantain was one of the first words you were able to pronounce. Perhaps it was that one time you tried it at a restaurant or a friend cooked it for you. Perhaps you have no memories at all because *gasp* you've never even tasted plantain. Whatever your story, I'm so pleased to welcome you into these pages.

If the whole concept of this cookbook hasn't given the game away yet, I am utterly and completely obsessed with plantain as an ingredient – much-loved and underrated as it is. We mostly fry it, boil it, roast it, turn it into chips, and that's that. This cookbook will show that there is so much more that can be done. Consider this my love letter to the humble fruit. You won't find anything too fancy in here (maybe we'll go gourmet for the next edition?) The recipes are accessible and easy to make, so anyone can pop into the shop, grab some plantain and get started immediately!

Why Vegan?
All the recipes in this cookbook are vegan (i.e. contain no animal products). I've been doing the whole vegan thing for nearly six years now, and absolutely loving it! I do it for my health, for the animals and for the planet. It's ramped up my passion for cooking, inspired me in endless ways, and led me on an exciting, food-filled journey.

Connect
I've been documenting bits of said journey on my blog The Vegan Nigerian. Head over for a visit. You'll find recipes, features, videos, vegan product reviews and a whole lot more to inspire you and brighten your day.

Website: www.vegannigerian.com
Instagram & Twitter: @vegannigerian
Facebook: The Vegan Nigerian

Plantain 101

Plantain is a starchy fruit that grows in different parts of the world, including Africa, Asia, South America, the Caribbean and the Pacific. Not to be mistaken with its mini-me lookalike, banana, plantains can be eaten at all stages of ripeness. Whether boiled, fried or roasted, they are flavoursome and ridiculously addictive.

Ripeness

Plantain skin always tells a story. Green, as you can probably guess, means it is still unripe. At this stage, it is great in soups, stews or as savoury chips. The next stage is bright yellow, when it is still firm but ripe enough to give you that little sweet kick. Once it turns yellow-black, you're entering super-sweet territory. The flesh is more tender, caramelises a lot easier and virtually melts in the mouth when cooked. The final stage of the almighty plantain is when it turns jet-black. At this point, you might think it's time to chuck it in the bin...but wait! It's luscious and perfect for adding to things like pancakes and puffy deep-fried buns (known in Nigeria as plantain mosa – visit my website for a recipe).

Where to Buy

If you live in South America and certain parts of Africa or Asia then chances are that you have access to more plantain than you can handle. Living in the West? Seek out and support the African/Caribbean food stores closest to you. And when in doubt, Google is your friend – you can order anything online!

Health Stuff

Plantains are a great source of vitamin C, vitamin A, potassium and dietary fibre. The natural sugars will give you boosts of energy without the crash and burn. Not bad at all.

The Basics

- Fried Plantain
- Baked Plantain Chips
- Boiled Plantain
- Roasted Plantain

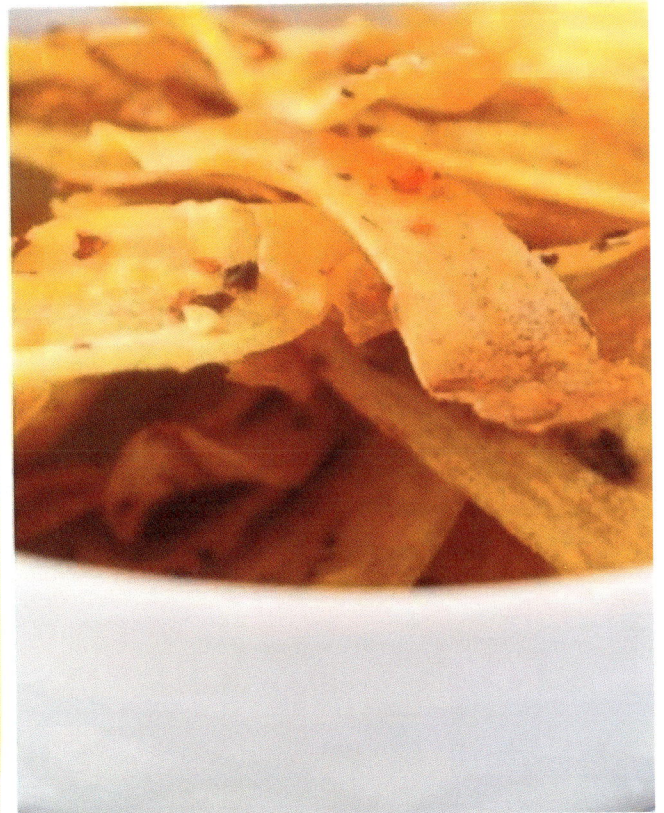

Fried Ripe Plantain (Dodo)

Directions

Serves 2

Ingredients

2 ripe plantains
100ml sunflower
oil
Pinch of salt

Cut off the top and tail of the plantains, then make a shallow incision along the length of the spine. Prise the skin open and remove the flesh.

Slice the plantain according to desired shape – diagonally, in rounds, strips or cubes.

Pour the oil into a wide frying pan. Heat the oil up on medium heat and fry the plantain, making sure not to overcrowd the pan. Turn the slices over after 3-4 minutes and fry the other side for another 2-3 minutes. The plantain should be golden brown on both sides.

Remove the slices from the pan and drain on some kitchen paper to remove excess oil. Serve warm as a side dish or starter.

Baked Plantain Chips

Serves 2

Ingredients

2 green plantains
2 tbsp sunflower oil
Salt, to taste

Directions

Preheat your oven to 200 degrees Celsius.

Peel the plantains and slice into thin strips or rounds using a mandolin slicer or sharp knife. Place the plantain in a bowl, add the sunflower oil and toss until evenly coated. Season with salt.

Line a baking tray with parchment paper and arrange a layer of the plantain slices. Bake for 20-25 minutes, or until golden brown and crispy. Leave to cool.

Plantain chips can also be made with ripe plantain for a less savoury version of the above. If you're low on time, plantain chips can also be made by deep frying in very hot oil – it's not as healthy, but it's a quicker process!

Boiled Plantain

Serves 2

Ingredients

2 ripe plantains
1 litre water

Directions

Rinse the plantains and cut off the tops and tails. Make a shallow incision along the length of the plantains. Slice each one into 3-4 large chunks, leaving the skin on.

Bring the water to a boil in a large saucepan. Add the plantain and cook for 15-20 minutes until soft. Drain and leave to cool slightly before peeling off the skins. Serve warm with a stew, salad or stir-fried vegetables.

Roasted Plantain

Serves 2

Ingredients

2 ripe plantains
2 tbsp sunflower oil

Directions

Preheat your oven to 180 degrees Celsius.

Peel the plantains and place whole or halved on a lined baking tray. Drizzle some sunflower oil over each plantain, to coat evenly. Bake for 15-20 minutes. Turn the plantains and bake for another 10-15 minutes until golden and tender. Serve warm as a snack with a handful of roasted peanuts, or as a side dish.

Breakfast & Brunch

- Scones
- Scramble/Frittata
- Smoothie Bowl
- Granola
- Porridge
- Breakfast Bars
- Pancakes
- Toast

Plantain Scones

Makes 12

Ingredients

300g plain flour
150g wholemeal flour
1 tsp baking powder
50g brown sugar
Pinch of salt
7 heap tbsp. vegan margarine
100ml non-dairy milk
1 tbsp vanilla extract
1 tbsp lemon juice
1 ripe plantain, mashed

Directions

Preheat your oven to 200 degrees Celsius.

Combine the flour, baking powder, sugar, salt and vegan margarine in a large mixing bowl. Rub the margarine into the flour mixture until it resembles breadcrumbs.

Combine all the wet ingredients and leave to stand for 5 minutes. Then add the wet ingredients to the dry ingredients slowly, folding the mixture lightly as you go until you have a sticky but firm dough. Do not knead or mix excessively.

Shape the dough into a 5cm thick circle on a heavily floured surface. Cut out the scones using a floured round pastry cutter. Reshape any leftover dough and keep cutting out the scones until you have used up all the dough. Place the scones on a lined baking tray and refrigerate for 30 minutes.

Bake for 15-20 minutes until risen and golden brown. Serve warm with jam, sweetened coconut cream, peanut butter or your favourite spread.

Plantain Frittata or Scramble

Serves 6

Ingredients

250g firm tofu
175g cooked butter beans
75ml water
4 tbsp nutritional yeast
4 tbsp corn flour
1 tsp turmeric powder
1 tsp salt
4 tbsp sunflower oil
1 ripe plantain, peeled &
cubed

Directions

Place the tofu butter beans, water, nutritional yeast, corn flour, turmeric and salt in a food processor and blend until smooth. Be patient with it. Stop and scrape down the sides at intervals.

Heat the sunflower oil in a large pan. Add the cubed plantain and all the chopped vegetables. Stir-fry for about 5-6 minutes until the vegetables are browned and cooked.

Combine the tofu mixture and stir fried vegetables in a mixing bowl. Fold in the chopped coriander. Transfer to a lightly greased springform pan. Bake at 200 degrees Celsius for 35-40 minutes until golden and set. Leave to cool completely before cutting into portions. Serve with a side of greens (you can never have too many greens, even at breakfast or brunch!)

Alternatively, use a fork to break up the frittata into a scramble. Serve warm with toast.

Banana & Mango Smoothie Bowl with Cinnamon & Coconut Plantain Crumbs

Serves 2

Ingredients

2 ripe bananas
1 mango
1 tbsp ground flaxseed
100ml non-dairy milk
5 ice cubes
200g sweet plantain chips
2 tbsp desiccated coconut
1 tsp cinnamon powder
Fresh fruits of your choice
Handful pumpkin seeds

Directions

Blend the bananas, mango, flaxseed, non-dairy milk and ice in a blender until smooth. Pour into serving bowls.

Crush the plantain chips and combine with the desiccated coconut and cinnamon powder. Sprinkle generously over the smoothies. Decorate with chopped fresh fruits and pumpkin seeds.

Spiced Plantain-Oat Granola

Serves 4

Ingredients

250g rolled oats
50g sunflower seeds
50g pumpkin seeds
50g cashews, chopped
50g raisins
85g plantain chips, crushed
1 tbsp ginger powder
1 tsp cinnamon
2 heap tbsp. vegan margarine
2 tbsp maple/rice syrup

Directions

Preheat your oven to 160 degrees Celsius.

Place all the ingredients in a large bowl and mix until well combined. You may need to use your fingers to rub in margarine.

Spread the mixture out on a lined baking tray. Bake for 10 minutes. Take the tray out and stir the mixture around to ensure that it bakes evenly. Bake for another 5 minutes. Leave to cool completely before serving with cold non-dairy milk or yoghurt.

Oat & Plantain Porridge

Serves 2

Ingredients

100g porridge oats
½ ripe plantain, peeled & chopped
150ml non-dairy milk
150ml water
1 tsp brown sugar
1 tsp nutmeg
Vegan yoghurt (coconut or soya)
Fresh or frozen fruits

Directions

Place the oats, plantain, milk, water, sugar and cinnamon in a saucepan. Bring to a boil then simmer on medium heat for 7-8 minutes, stirring occasionally.

Serve in bowls with a generous spoonful of coconut yoghurt and mixed fruit of your choice.

Sweet Plantain, Peanut & Apple Breakfast Bars

Makes 20

Ingredients

250g oats
250ml non-dairy milk
2 tbsp brown sugar
1 ripe plantain, mashed
2 apples, grated
3 tbsp desiccated coconut
2 tbsp unsalted peanut butter
1 tsp mixed spice

Directions

Preheat your oven to 180 degrees Celsius.

Place the oats, milk and sugar in a bowl and allow to sit for 15 minutes. Add the mashed plantain, grated apple, desiccated coconut, peanut butter and mixed spice. Mix until well combined.

Line a medium-sized rectangular baking tray with parchment paper and pour in the mixture. Bake for 40-45 minutes until firm and golden brown. Leave to cool completely before slicing into bars.

Store for up to four days in an airtight container. If you're allergic to nuts, replace the peanut butter with vegan margarine or sunflower seed butter.

Choc Chip Plantain Pancakes

Serves 2

Ingredients

½ very ripe plantain
200ml non-dairy milk
1 tsp vanilla extract
100g self-raising flour
½ tsp baking powder
25g sugar
Handful dark chocolate chips
Sunflower oil
Maple syrup, to serve

Directions

In a large mixing bowl, mash the plantain and whisk in the non-dairy milk and vanilla extract.

Mix the flour, baking powder and sugar in another bowl and make a well in the centre. Pour in the liquid mixture and stir until well combined. Fold in the chocolate chips.

Heat a small layer of sunflower oil in a frying fan. Drop spoonfuls of the batter into the pan, spreading to desired thickness. Brown on one side for 3-4 minutes then flip over and brown the other side for a further 1-2 minutes. Repeat the process until you have used up all the batter. Serve warm with a generous drizzle of maple syrup and more chocolate chips.

Smoky Plantain, Mushroom & Avocado on Toast

Serves 2

Ingredients

4 slices of bread, toasted
2 ripe avocados
2 tbsp lemon juice
3 tbsp sunflower oil
1 ripe plantain, peeled & sliced
1 red onion, chopped
100g mushrooms, chopped
1 tsp smoked paprika
Salt and pepper, to taste

Directions

Mash the avocados and mix in the lemon juice and a pinch of salt. Set aside.

Heat the sunflower oil in a large frying pan and add the plantain and onion. Cook for 5 minutes until the plantain is browned and the onions are slightly translucent. Add the mushrooms and stir-fry for another 3 minutes. Season with smoked paprika, salt and pepper.

Assemble the toast, starting with a generous spread of mashed avocado and a spoonful or two of the fried plantains and mushrooms.

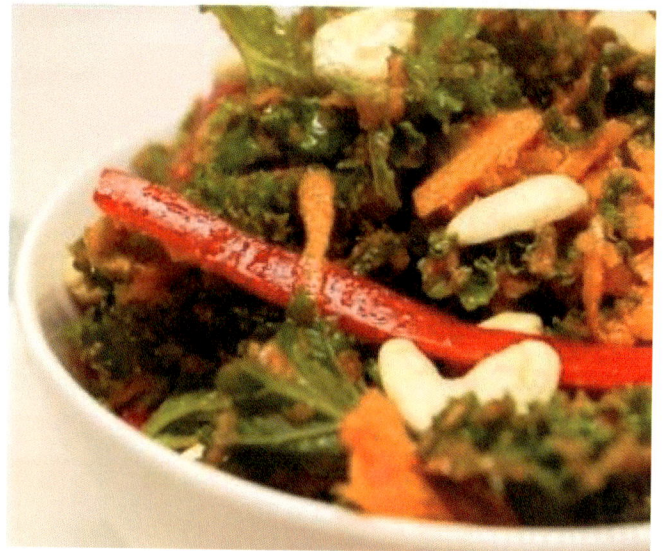

Snacks & Light Meals

- Wedges + Garlic Mayo
- Pita Wrap
- Cauliflower wings
- Fully-loaded Chips
- Kale Salad
- Tofu Spiralised Salad
- Sweetcorn Fritters
- Couscous Salad
- Sweet Potato/Bean Pies

Crusted Plantain Wedges with Roasted Garlic Mayo

Serves 4

Ingredients

For the wedges:
2 semi-ripe plantains
3 tbsp corn meal
1 tsp chilli powder
1 tsp garlic powder
1 tsp dried thyme
Salt, to taste
1 tbsp sunflower oil

For the mayo:
2 heads garlic
200g silken tofu
3 tbsp lime juice
3 tbsp sunflower oil
Salt and pepper, to taste

Directions

Peel and slice the plantains into thick wedges. Place in a bowl and toss with corn meal, chilli flakes, garlic powder, thyme and salt until well coated.

Arrange the wedges on a lined baking tray, drizzle with sunflower oil and bake for 30-35 minutes at 180 degrees Celsius until crispy.

Cut the tops off the garlic and coat the bulbs with sunflower oil before wrapping completely in foil. Bake alongside the wedges for 25 minutes. The garlic should get soft and caramelised. Leave to cool before squeezing out the garlic from the skins.

To make the garlic mayo, place the roasted garlic, tofu, lime juice and sunflower oil in a blender and blend until smooth. Season with salt and pepper.

Serve the wedges warm with the garlic mayo.

Plantain Pita Sandwich

Serves 2

Ingredients

2 tbsp sunflower oil
1 ripe plantain, diced
1 red bell pepper, cut into strips
1 courgette, sliced
Pita bread
Red pepper hummus
Salad greens

Directions

Heat the sunflower oil in a large frying pan and add the diced plantain. Cook until the plantain is golden brown on all sides. Add the peppers and courgette and cook for a couple of minutes until they have softened a little. Transfer to a bowl.

Warm up and slice your pita bread in half and fill with red pepper hummus, salad greens and a generous spoonful or two of the plantain and vegetable mix.

Plantain-Cauliflower Bites

Serves 4

Ingredients

1 large cauliflower
1 ripe plantain, peeled
2 stalks spring onions
½ brown onion
2 tbsp flaxseeds
2 tbsp fine corn meal
1 tbsp wholemeal flour
2 garlic cloves
1 tsp cumin
1 tsp salt
1 tsp lime zest
Juice of 1 lime
2 tbsp sunflower oil

Directions

Preheat your oven to 200 degrees Celsius.

Cut the cauliflower into bite-size florets.

Place the plantain, spring onions, onions, flaxseeds, corn meal, wholemeal flour, garlic, cumin, salt, lime zest, lime juice and sunflower oil in a food processor. Blend for 2-3 minutes until you have a thick, smooth batter. Transfer to a bowl. Add the cauliflower florets and toss to coat evenly.

Line a baking sheet with parchment paper and lightly grease the surface. Spread the cauliflower out on a single layer. Bake for 30 minutes until golden brown.

Serve the bites warm with your favourite dips and sauces.

Fully-Loaded Plantain Chips

Serves 4

Ingredients

Plantain chips (see page 11)
Tomato sauce
Chilli powder
Vegan cheese, grated
Avocado, cubed
Tomatoes, chopped
Black olives, sliced
Fresh coriander, chopped
Sunflower seeds
Salt and pepper, to taste

Directions

To put this simple snack together, spread the plantain chips on a lined baking tray and top with the tomato sauce, chilli powder and vegan cheese. Grill for about 5 minutes until the cheese begins to melt. Then simply top with the rest of the ingredients.

Massaged Kale Salad with a Fiery Plantain Dressing

Serves 2

Ingredients

250g kale
Handful grated carrot
1 red bell pepper, sliced
½ ripe plantain, boiled
½ scotch bonnet pepper
100g sun-dried tomatoes
2 tbsp sunflower oil
25ml cider vinegar
25ml water
Salt and pepper, to taste
Cashew nuts

Directions

Place the kale, carrot and red pepper in a large salad bowl.

To make the dressing, place the boiled plantain, scotch bonnet pepper, sun-dried tomatoes, sunflower oil, cider vinegar and water in a blender and blend until smooth and creamy. Add to the salad and 'massage' until well combined. This will help to soften the kale leaves. Season with a dash of salt and pepper, if needed. Throw on a handful of cashew nuts.

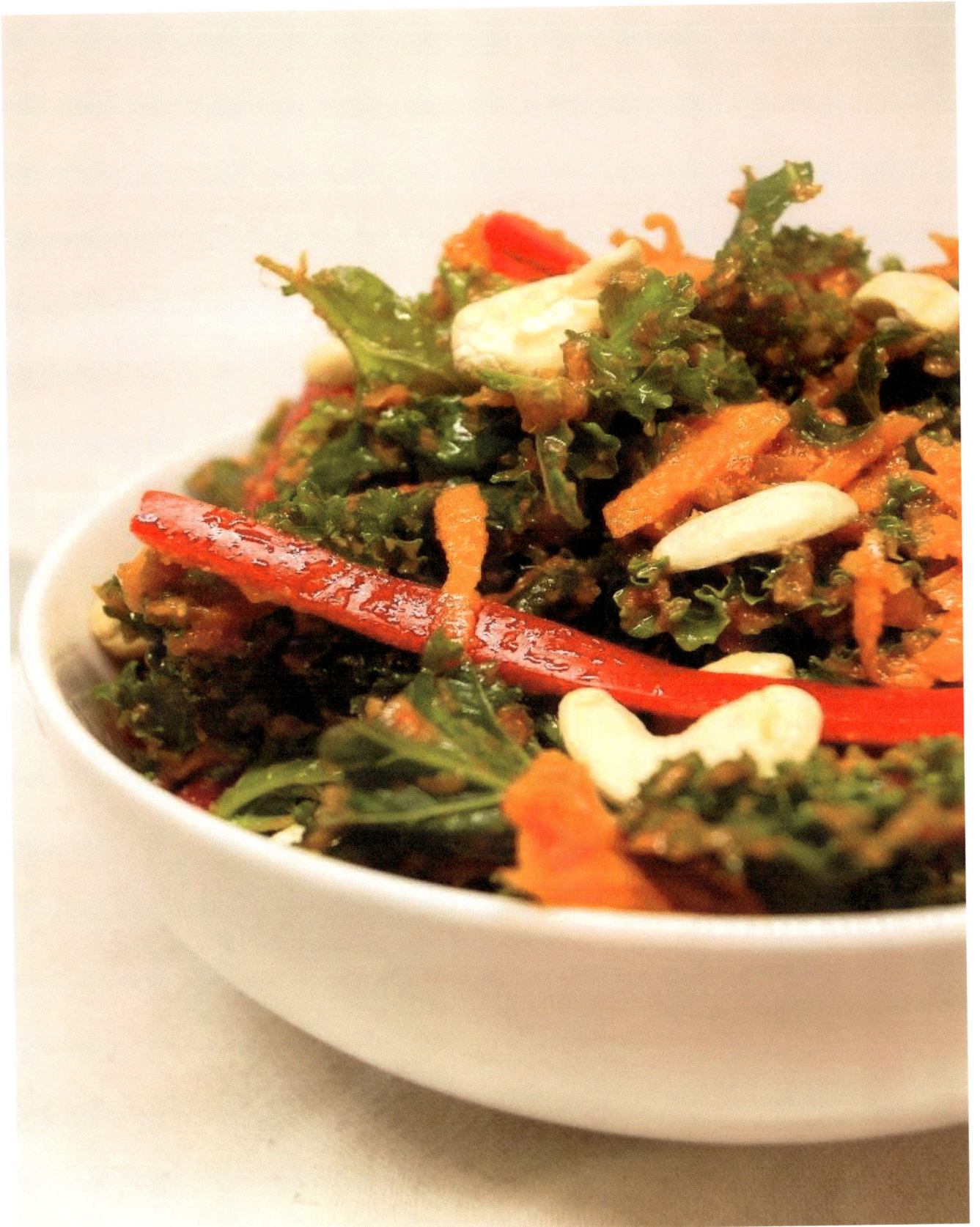

Marinated Tofu & Plantain Spiralised Salad

Serves 2

Ingredients

250g extra firm tofu, cubed
1 ripe plantain, cut into batons
2 tbsp crushed ginger
2 garlic cloves, minced
4 tbsp siracha sauce
2 tbsp sesame oil
5 tbsp light soy sauce
2 courgettes
4 carrots
100g cherry tomatoes, halved
1 lime

Directions

To make the marinade, whisk together the ginger, garlic, rice vinegar, sesame oil and soy sauce. In a large bowl, toss the tofu and plantain with 3/4 of the marinade mixture. Leave to stand for at least 30 minutes.

Arrange the marinated tofu and plantain on a lined baking tray and bake at 200 degrees Celsius for 20-25 minutes. Leave to cool.

Use a spiralizer or julienne peeler to spiralise the carrots and courgettes. Arrange in a large salad bowl. Add the marinated tofu and plantain. Top with cherry tomatoes. Add some fresh lime juice to the remaining marinade and drizzle on top of the salad.

Plantain & Sweetcorn Fritters

Makes 18-20

Ingredients

3 heap tbsp. wholegrain flour

1 tsp salt

1 tsp fennel seeds

1 tsp chilli flakes

1 tbsp flaxseeds

125ml water

130g sweetcorn

1 plantain, peeled & chopped

1 red onion, chopped

2 garlic cloves, chopped

Sunflower oil

Directions

Combine the flour, salt, fennel seeds, chilli flakes, flaxseeds and water in a large mixing bowl to form a batter. Don't over-mix.

Add the sweetcorn, plantain, onion and garlic clove to the batter and mix to combine. Let the batter sit for 10 minutes.

Heat about 4 tbsp sunflower oil in a large non-stick pan. Add the fritters in tablespoonfuls – be careful not to overcrowd the pan. Fry for 4-5 minutes on one side until deep golden brown. Gently turn them over, reduce the heat to medium and fry for another 3-4 minutes. Repeat until you have used up all the batter. You may need to add a little bit more oil to the pan as you go along.

Serve hot or warm on their own, with a side salad or with dips and sauces.

Fruity Plantain & Mixed Veg Couscous

Serves 2

Ingredients

1 plantain, peeled & diced
1 red bell pepper, diced
1 yellow bell pepper, diced
2 carrots, diced
2 tbsp coconut oil
170g couscous
300ml boiling hot water
25g dried apricots, chopped
25g sultanas or raisins
Handful chopped parsley
Handful chopped coriander
Salt and pepper, to taste
Pomegranate seeds

Directions

Toss the diced plantain, bell peppers and carrot with coconut oil and spread on a lined baking tray. Bake for 25 minutes at 180 degrees Celsius.

Prepare the couscous by pouring over the boiling hot water. Cover and leave to stand for 5 minutes. Use a fork to fluff up the couscous. Add the baked vegetables, apricots, sultanas and chopped mixed herbs. Season with salt and pepper. Sprinkle some pomegranate seeds over the top for an extra splash of colour.

Plantain, Sweet Potato & Kidney Bean Pies

Serves 4

Ingredients

4 tbsp sunflower oil
1 plantain, peeled & chopped
100g red kidney beans, cooked
50g sweetcorn
50g peas
150g sweet potatoes, cooked
1 tbsp tomato paste
Handful chopped parsley
Salt, to taste
Ready-roll shortcrust pastry

Directions

Preheat your oven to 180 degrees Celsius.

Heat the sunflower oil in a large pan and fry the chopped plantain until golden brown. Add the beans, sweetcorn, peas, sweet potatoes and tomato paste. Stir-fry for 3-4 minutes, adding a little water if the mixture is too dry, and then add the chopped parsley. Season with salt.

Divide the pastry into 4 squares. Spoon some of the filling onto one side of the circle, leaving some space around the edge. Fold over the pastry to enclose the filling, use a fork to press and seal the edges, and to make small holes through the top. Repeat this process with the rest of the pastry and filling.

Place each pie on a lined baking tray, brush with a little oil or non-dairy milk and bake for 25-30 minutes until golden brown.

Hearty Meals

- Creamy Spaghetti
- Herby Mash
- Fried Rice
- Burger
- Pottage
- Pot Pies
- Quiche
- Curry
- Dumpling Soup
- Lasagne
- Oven Bake

Creamy Pasta with Crispy Plantain

Serves 4

Ingredients

1 ripe plantain, diced

3 tbsp fine corn meal

2 tbsp sunflower oil

Handful coriander, chopped

500ml water

400g spaghetti

2 tbsp coconut oil

1 red onion, chopped

3 cloves garlic, chopped

100g mushrooms, chopped

100g green beans

250ml tinned coconut milk

Salt and pepper, to taste

1 tsp dried sage

1 tsp crushed chilli flakes

Directions

Toss the plantain and corn meal together. Heat the sunflower oil in a pan and fry the plantain until golden brown. Add the coriander at the last moment. Set aside.

Bring the water to a boil and add the spaghetti. Cook for 5 minutes until al dente. Drain.

Heat the coconut oil in a large pan and add the onion and garlic. Sautee until the onion is translucent then add the mushrooms and green beans. Stir in the coconut milk, season with salt, pepper, dried sage and chilli flakes, and bring to a boil. Add the spaghetti, reduce to medium heat and simmer uncovered for a few minutes until most of the liquid is absorbed. Serve hot with the crispy plantain and coriander over the top.

Herby Green Plantain Mash with Vegan Sausages

Serves 2

Ingredients

2 green plantains
500ml water
2 tbsp coconut oil
50ml coconut milk
2 tbsp chopped mint
2 tbsp chopped coriander
1 tbsp chopped parsley
Salt and pepper, to taste
4 vegan sausages

Directions

Peel and slice each plantain into 4-5 pieces. Place in a pot of boiling water and cook for 15 minutes, or until tender. Drain, add the coconut oil and milk, and mash with a fork until chunky-smooth. Fold in the chopped herbs. Season with salt and pepper.

Serve the plantain hot with a side of vegan sausages.

Plantain Fried Rice

Serves 4

Ingredients

2 tbsp coconut oil

1 plantain, diced

3 spring onions, chopped

2 carrots, chopped

50g frozen peas

400g cooked golden basmati rice

4 tbsp light soy sauce

Directions

Heat the coconut oil in a large frying pan and add the diced plantain. Fry until golden brown. Add the spring onions and peas. Stir-fry for 2-3 minutes. Add the cooked rice and season with soy sauce. Stir-fry for another 5 minutes and serve hot.

Baked Plantain Burgers

Serves 4

Ingredients

100g red lentils
1 ripe plantain, mashed
½ red onion, chopped
2 carrots, grated
3 tbsp sunflower oil
1 tsp cumin
1 tbsp dried mixed herbs
Salt, to taste

Directions

Preheat your oven to 200 degrees Celsius.

Cook the red lentils in lightly salted water until it is soft, mushy and most of the water has evaporated. You will need to keep a close eye and stir constantly to make sure that it doesn't stick to the bottom of the pot. Add a little water at a time if the lentils are not fully cooked before the water dries out. The final result should resemble a thick paste.

Place the mashed plantain, onion and carrot in a large mixing bowl. Mix in the cooked lentils then add the sunflower oil, cumin and mixed herbs. Season with salt.

Form the mixture into four round burgers on a lined baking tray (don't worry about the mixture appearing too wet – it will firm up nicely in the oven). Bake for 30 minutes, then turn each burger over and bake for a further 7 minutes. Serve with a side salad or in a burger bun with your favourite sauce and toppings.

Beans & Plantain Pottage

Serves 4

Ingredients

400g brown or black-eyed beans
1 red bell pepper
1 tin plum tomatoes
1 scotch bonnet pepper
3 cloves garlic
2 yellow plantains, sliced
½ red onion, sliced
2 tbsp sustainable palm oil
Salt, to taste

Directions

Soak the beans for a few hours or overnight, if possible. Drain and cook with about 2 litres of water for 90 minutes or until tender and most of the water is absorbed. Keep a close eye on it and add more water during the cooking time if needed.

Blend the red pepper, tomatoes, scotch bonnet and garlic until smooth. Add to the beans, along with the sliced plantain, onion and palm oil. Season with salt. Simmer on medium heat for 20 minutes. Serve hot.

Plantain & Mushroom Pot Pies

Serves 2

Ingredients

2 tbsp coconut oil
1 ripe plantain, chopped
1 red onion, chopped
100g mushrooms, chopped
2 carrots, chopped
2 cloves garlic, chopped
1 stalk celery, chopped
100g sweetcorn
2 tbsp corn flour
100ml water
Salt and pepper
1 sheet ready-roll puff pastry
4 tbsp non-dairy milk

Directions

Preheat your oven to 200 degrees Celsius.

Heat the coconut oil in a large frying pan. Fry the chopped plantain until browned then remove from the pan. Add the chopped onions, mushrooms, carrots, garlic, celery and sweetcorn to the pan. Stir-fry for 5 minutes on medium heat then cover with water. Gently stir in the corn flour and season with salt and pepper. Add the plantain to the pan and simmer for a few minutes until the sauce just starts to thicken.

Roll out the puff pastry and use a cookie cutter to cut out circles that are big enough to cover your ramekins.

Spoon the plantain and mushroom mixture into ramekins and cover each one with a circle of pastry. Use a fork to poke holes in the pastry and brush the tops with a little non-dairy milk.

Place the ramekins on a baking tray and bake for about 20 minutes, or until the pastry is puffy and golden brown. Allow to rest for a few minutes before serving.

Plantain, Sun-Dried Tomato & Spinach Quiche

Serves 8

Ingredients

For the pastry:
150g wholegrain flour
150g plain flour
130g coconut oil
Pinch of salt
Approx. 100ml cold water

For the filling:
500g silken tofu
1 tbsp sunflower oil
3 garlic cloves
4 tbsp nutritional yeast
3 tbsp corn flour
1 tbsp dried sage
1 tsp dried thyme
Salt and pepper, to taste
1 red onion, chopped
100g sun-dried tomatoes
200g spinach, chopped,

Directions

Preheat your oven to 200 degrees Celsius.

To make the pastry, add the flour and salt to a mixing bowl. Rub in the coconut oil until the mixture resembles breadcrumbs. Slowly add the water to the flour, one tablespoon at a time, until you have a soft dough. Chill in the fridge for about 30 minutes.

Roll out the dough on a floured surface to a 1/2 inch thick circle and line a quiche tin. Leave some pastry hanging over the edge of the tin (the pastry will shrink during baking). Poke the base of the pastry with a fork, cover the entire pastry with baking paper and fill the base with dry beans or rice. Blind bake for 10 minutes, then remove the baking paper and beans/rice. Bake for a further 5 minutes.

In a food processor, add the silken tofu, sunflower oil, garlic cloves and nutritional yeast. Blend until smooth. Transfer to a large bowl and add the dried sage, salt and pepper. Fold in the chopped onions, sun-dried tomatoes and spinach. Pour the filling into the partially-baked pastry case and arrange the sliced plantain over the top until completely covered. Brush the surface with a little oil and bake for 25-30 minutes, or until golden brown. Leave to stand for 10 minutes before serving.

Aromatic Plantain-Vegetable Curry

Serves 4

Ingredients

2 tbsp sunflower oil

1 red onion, chopped

1 green plantain, chopped

1 tbsp minced ginger

2-3 bay leaves

1 tbsp curry powder

1 scotch bonnet pepper, halved

300ml coconut milk

3 carrots, sliced

50g green beans

150g broccoli

50g peas

50g sweetcorn

Salt, to taste

Directions

Heat the sunflower oil in a large saucepan over medium heat. Add the onion, plantain, minced ginger and bay leaves, and cook for 3-4 minutes. Add the curry powder, scotch bonnet and coconut milk. Add the plantain and leave to simmer on medium heat for about 10 minutes. Add the rest of the vegetables and cook for a further 5 minutes. Season with salt. Serve hot with rice or bread.

Plantain Dumpling Soup

Serves 2

Ingredients

For the soup:

2 tbsp sunflower oil

1 red onion, chopped

2 garlic cloves, chopped

1 carrot, shredded

250g yam or sweet potatoes, chopped

2 celery stalks, chopped

100g frozen peas

1.5 litres water

1 scotch bonnet pepper, quartered

1 tbsp season-all

1 tsp oregano

Salt, to taste

For the dumplings:

1 overripe plantain, mashed

3 tbsp wholegrain flour

¼ tsp baking powder

1 tsp chilli flakes

1 tsp salt

Directions

To make the soup, heat the sunflower oil in a large soup pot over medium heat. Add the chopped onion, garlic and carrot. Stir-fry for about 3-4 minutes then add the yam/sweet potatoes, celery and frozen peas. Cover with the water and add the scotch bonnet, season-all, oregano and salt. Simmer on medium-low heat for about 20-25 minutes.

To make the dumplings, mix the mashed plantain, flour, baking powder, chilli flakes and salt to form a thick batter. Use a tablespoon to scoop and drop round dumplings into the soup. Cook the soup for another 10 minutes on medium heat. Serve piping hot.

Plantain Lasagne

Serves 4

Ingredients

6 ripe plantains
Sunflower oil
3 garlic cloves, chopped
1 tsp chilli powder
1 tsp dried mixed herbs
1 tsp smoked paprika
300ml tomato sauce
125g cooked red lentils
4 tbsp vegan margarine
8 tbsp plain flour
400ml non-dairy milk
Salt and pepper, to taste
Vegan cheese, optional

Directions

Peel and slice the plantains horizontal into 4-5 thick strips.

Heat a few tablespoons of sunflower oil in a large frying pan and fry the plantain in batches, browning the strips on both sides. Drain on kitchen paper and set aside.

Add a tablespoon of sunflower oil to a large saucepan and add the garlic, chilli, mixed herbs, smoked paprika, tomato sauce and lentils. Simmer on medium-low heat for about 12 minutes until the lentils start to soften.

Make a white sauce by melting the vegan margarine in a saucepan. Add the flour and stir vigorously to combine. Add the non-dairy milk slowly, whisking as you go along. Allow to bubble and thicken on low heat for a couple of minutes.

Assemble the lasagne by lining the bottom of a greased medium-sized oven dish with fried plantain. Spread a thin layer of the tomato-lentil sauce over the top and then drizzle over some of the white sauce. Add another layer of fried plantain and repeat the process until all the ingredients are used up. If desired, add some vegan cheese between the layers and sprinkle a little over the top.

Bake at 180 degrees Celsius for 25-30 minutes. Serve hot.

Broccoli, Tomato & Plantain Bake

Serves 2

Ingredients

1 ripe plantain, chopped
500g broccoli florets
4 tomatoes, quartered
4 tbsp sunflower oil
1 tbsp chilli flakes
Salt and pepper, to taste

Directions

Preheat your oven to 200 degrees Celsius.

Toss all the ingredients together in a large bowl and then spread them out on a lined baking tray. Bake for 25-30 minutes until the plantain is golden brown and the broccoli starts to crisp around the edges. Serve hot or warm.

Desserts & Bakes

- Chocolate/Coconut Discs
- Caramel Energy Balls
- Peanut Butter Energy Balls
- Chocolate Fudge Cake
- Fruit Loaf
- Mixed Berry Mosa
- Cupcakes
- Walnut Pastries
- Mocha Cookies
- Carrot Cupcakes

Chocolate & Toasted Coconut Plantain Discs

Serves 4

Ingredients

1 ripe but firm plantain
2 tbsp coconut oil
Ground nutmeg
100g dark chocolate
50g toasted desiccated coconut

Directions

Peel and cut the plantain into thick round circles. Flatten each one gently with a fork to form a crushed disc. Place on a baking tray and brush both sides with some coconut oil. Sprinkle some nutmeg over the top. Bake for 20 minutes at 200 degrees Celsius then turn each one over and bake for a further 10 minutes. Leave to cool on a wire rack.

Melt the dark chocolate in the microwave at 20 second intervals. Be careful not to burn the chocolate. Stir until fully melted.

Dip each disc halfway in the melted chocolate. Lay each one on a tray lined with baking paper. Sprinkle the chocolate covered ends with the toasted coconut. Chill for half an hour until the chocolate sets.

If you have any melted chocolate left over, you can use as an extra dipping sauce.

Caramel Plantain Chip Energy Balls

Makes 20

Ingredients

100g sweet plantain chips
50g shredded coconut
170g cashew nuts
300g soft dates
1 tbsp coconut oil
Pinch of salt

Directions

Place all the ingredients in a food processor and blend until it forms a firm dough. You may need to scrape down the sides at intervals and add a tablespoon or two of water to bring the mixture together. Transfer to a bowl.

Shape into bite-sized balls by pressing and rolling between your palms.

Store in an airtight container and keep refrigerated for up to two weeks.

Peanut Butter & Plantain Chip Energy Balls

Makes 20

Ingredients

250g oats
100g unripe plantain chips
2 tbsp chia seeds
4 tbsp unsalted peanut butter
5 tbsp maple syrup
Pinch of salt

Directions

Place all the ingredients in a food processor and blend until it forms a firm dough. You may need to scrape down the sides at intervals and add a tablespoon or two of water to bring the mixture together. Transfer to a bowl.

Shape into bite-sized balls by pressing and rolling between your palms.

Store in an airtight container and keep refrigerated for up to two weeks.

Plantain Chocolate Fudge Cake

Serves 10

Ingredients

100g dark chocolate
200ml non-dairy milk
125ml sunflower oil
1 tbsp vanilla extract
3 very ripe plantains, mashed
100g plain flour
100g wholemeal flour
100g cocoa powder
250g brown sugar
1 tbsp baking powder

Directions

Preheat your oven to 160 degrees Celsius.

Place the dark chocolate and non-dairy milk in a microwavable bowl and microwave for 30 seconds. Stir and microwave for another 20 seconds until the chocolate has melted completely. Transfer to a large mixing bowl and whisk in the oil, vanilla and mashed plantain.

Mix the flours, cocoa powder, brown sugar and baking powder in another large mixing bowl and make a well in the centre. Add the wet ingredients slowly, stirring as you go until you have a smooth, thick batter.

Lightly grease a cake tin with vegan margarine and dust with a little flour. Pour in the cake batter. Bake for 30-35 minutes, then leave to stand for a few minutes. Serve warm with a scoop of non-dairy ice cream.

Fruity Plantain Loaf

Serves 6-8

Ingredients

2 ripe plantains, mashed
75ml sunflower oil
100ml non-dairy milk
75g brown sugar
150g self-raising flour
100g wholemeal flour
1 tsp baking powder
2 tsp mixed spice
1 tsp ginger powder
50g dried mixed fruits

Directions

Preheat your oven to 160 degrees Celsius.

Whisk the mashed plantains, sunflower oil and non-dairy milk together.

Add all the dry ingredients to a large mixing bowl and make a well in the centre. Pour in the liquid ingredients, stirring slowly as you go along.

Bake in a greased or lined loaf tin for 40-45 minutes. Use a toothpick or skewer to check if it is cooked in the middle. If it comes out clean then you are good to go. Serve with warm custard or whipped coconut cream.

Plantain & Mixed Berry Mosa

Serves 8

Ingredients

2 very ripe plantains
4 heap tbsp. self-raising flour
2 tbsp fine corn meal
Handful frozen mixed berries
Sunflower oil
Cinnamon powder
Brown sugar (optional)

Directions

Peel and mash the plantains in a large mixing bowl. Add the flour and corn meal and mix to form a sticky dough. Carefully fold in the mixed berries.

Heat enough sunflower oil for deep frying in a large pan. Fry the mosa in batches (by the tablespoonful) until golden brown. Drain on some kitchen paper to remove excess oil. Dust with cinnamon and brown sugar for extra sweetness.

Plantain Chip Cupcakes

Makes 12

Ingredients

250g self-raising flour
150g caster sugar
100g plantain chips, crushed
100ml sunflower oil
250ml non-dairy milk
1 tsp vanilla extract

Directions

Preheat your oven to 180 degrees Celsius.

Combine the flour, sugar and crushed plantain chips in a large mixing bowl.

Whisk the sunflower oil, non-dairy milk and vanilla together in a separate bowl or jug, then add to the dry ingredients. Mix gently to form a smooth batter.

Line a cupcake tin with cupcake holders and scoop some batter into each holder, filling 3/4 way full.

Bake for 25-30 minutes until risen and golden brown. Use a skewer or toothpick to check the centre of each cupcake – it should come out clean. Allow the cupcakes to cool completely before serving.

Got some vegan buttercream handy? Pipe some over the top of your cupcakes and garnish with sweet, crunchy plantain chips for a simple but classy finish. Buttercream can be made by combining 3 parts icing sugar with 1 part vegan margarine and a few teaspoons of vegan milk to lighten the mixture.

Maple-Glazed Plantain & Walnut Pastries

Serves 4

Ingredients

Ready-roll puff pastry
1 ripe plantain, boiled
Handful walnuts, chopped
1 tsp nutmeg
Maple syrup

Directions

Preheat your oven to 200 degrees Celsius.

Mash the boiled plantain to form a smooth puree. Fold in the chopped walnuts and add the nutmeg.

Cut the puff pastry into four 12cm by 12cm squares. Spoon the plantain and walnut mix into the centre of each piece and pinch two of the opposite ends to the centre to partially encase the filling.

Place each pastry on a lined baking tray, brush with maple syrup and bake for 20 minutes until golden brown. Leave to cool on a wire rack, drizzle with more maple syrup and chopped walnuts before serving.

Mocha Plantain Chip Cookies

Makes 18-20

Ingredients

200g spelt flour
100g cocoa powder
1 tsp baking powder
150g brown sugar
100g sweet plantain chips
Pinch of salt
5 tbsp vegan margarine
2 tbsp instant coffee
50ml non-dairy milk
1 tsp vanilla extract

Directions

Preheat your oven to 180 degrees Celsius.

Place the spelt flour, cocoa powder, baking powder, brown sugar, crushed plantain chips, vegan margarine and salt in a large mixing bowl. Use your fingers to rub the margarine into the mixture until it looks crumbly.

Dissolve the instant coffee in hot non-dairy milk and leave to cool. Add to the mixing bowl, along with the vanilla. Combine to form a dough.

Line baking trays with parchment paper and drop the cookie dough in heap spoonfuls, leaving space between each one. Flatten the cookies with your fingers or with the back of a fork. Bake for 15-20 minutes and allow to cool on a wire rack.

Store in an airtight container for up to five days.

Plantain & Carrot Cupcakes

Makes 12

Ingredients

200ml non-dairy milk
80ml sunflower oil
2 tsp vanilla extract
150g self-raising flour
50g wholemeal flour
120g brown sugar
2 tsp baking powder
2 tsp cinnamon
1 tsp nutmeg
1 ripe plantain, chopped
100g grated carrot
50g dried fruits and nuts

Directions

Preheat your oven to 180 degrees Celsius.

Whisk the non-dairy milk, oil and vanilla together. Set aside.

Combine the rest of the dry ingredients in a large mixing bowl and make a well in the centre. Stir in the wet ingredients to form a cake batter.

Line a cupcake tin with cupcake holders and scoop some batter into each holder, filling 3/4 of the way up.

Bake for 25-30 minutes until risen and golden brown. Use a skewer or toothpick to check the centre of each cupcake – it should come out clean. Allow the cupcakes to cool completely before serving.

Keep in Touch!

FOR MORE RECIPES & INSPIRATION

FOLLOW ME ON:

INSTAGRAM

TWITTER

FACEBOOK

YOUTUBE

@VeganNigerian

www.vegannigerian.com

Printed in Poland
by Amazon Fulfillment
Poland Sp. z o.o., Wrocław